TABLE OF CONTENTS

INTRODUCTION: LOVE IN THE DIGITAL AGE

The digital age has transformed how people connect, form relationships, and fall in love. Dating apps and online platforms have created opportunities for millions, allowing people to meet others they may never have crossed paths with in everyday life. But with this convenience comes complexity—navigating dating app algorithms, crafting appealing profiles, and keeping genuine interactions, and avoiding crazy serial killers require effort and understanding.

This little book is designed to help you master the art of online dating, blending practical advice with insights into the algorithms that drive the digital dating world. By using technology and refining your approach, you'll discover how to optimize your experience and make meaningful connections. I've dated hundreds of men online and know what I'm writing about.

CREATING YOUR OWN LOVE ALGORITHM

Part 1: Decoding the Algorithm

Dating app algorithms analyze user behavior, preferences, and activity to suggest matches. Think of them as behind-the-scenes concierge sorting through profiles to find your best fit. To improve the results, actively engage with the app. Log in regularly, swipe thoughtfully, and respond to messages promptly.

Refine your preferences to align with your genuine desires. While broad filters might increase your options, narrowing them can yield better compatibility. Timing matters too—engaging during peak hours (evenings and weekends) boosts your visibility.

Finally, balance your reliance on technology with proactive social interactions. Attend events or join groups aligned with your interests to broaden your chances of meeting someone compatible.

UNDERSTANDING DATING APP ALGORITHMS: EXPLAINED WITH CODE

Part 1: Overview of Dating App Algorithms

Dating app algorithms aim to create compatibility by using user-provided data and behavioral insights. They analyze factors like location, preferences, and interaction history to suggest matches with the highest potential for connection. By continuously learning from user activity, these algorithms refine their accuracy over time.

For example, most apps prioritize engagement frequency, so users who log in regularly and interact often have higher visibility. Keywords in profiles are also critical, as they inform the system about shared interests and alignments. To demystify this further, let's explore a simplified version of an algorithm in code form.

Part 2: Example Code for Matching Logic

```
class User:
    def __init__(self, name, age, location,
interests):
        self.name = name
        self.age = age
        self.location = location
        self.interests = interests

# Example user profiles
user1 = User("Alex", 29, "NYC", ["hiking",
"music", "cooking"])
user2 = User("Taylor", 30, "NYC", ["traveling",
"hiking", "art"])
```

```
# Match scoring function
def calculate_match_score(user1, user2):
    score = 0

    # Compare location
    if user1.location == user2.location:
        score += 20

    # Compare interests
    shared_interests =
set(user1.interests).intersection(set(user2.int
erests))
    score += len(shared_interests) * 10

    # Return compatibility score
    return score

# Calculate the match score
match_score = calculate_match_score(user1,
user2)
print(f"Match Score: {match_score}")
```

Part 3: How to Influence Results

Understanding this simplified algorithm can help you tailor your approach:

1. **Broaden Your Location Radius**: Expanding the distance you're willing to match increases the pool of potential matches. For instance, adjusting your settings to include neighboring cities can offer more opportunities to meet individuals who align with your preferences. This tactic is particularly helpful for those in smaller towns or niche communities.
2. **Perfect Interests in Your Profile**: Align your hobbies and preferences with the type of person you want to attract. If you're looking for someone adventurous, highlight activities like "rock climbing" or "backpacking." This creates keyword matches in the algorithm, increasing the likelihood

of connecting with individuals who share those traits.

3. **Stay Active and Consistent**: Logging in daily, responding to messages promptly, and engaging with profiles ensure the algorithm views you as a highly active user. High activity boosts your visibility to other users and positions your profile higher in search results.

4. **Leverage Super Likes or Premium Features**: Using paid features during peak times (usually evenings) significantly boosts your profile's visibility. These tools signal to the algorithm that you're prioritizing a specific connection, making it more likely to show your profile to high-quality matches.

5. **Experiment and Adjust Regularly**: Periodically update your profile photos, bios, and preferences. This keeps your profile fresh and signals active engagement, which algorithms reward. Small changes, like updating your "About Me" section to reflect current interests, can make a big impact in attracting the right matches.

Tailoring Your Profile to Influence Results

The key to mastering the algorithm lies in the details of your profile and the way you interact with the app. If you're looking for a specific type of match—say, a "bad boy" type—you can tailor your profile and interactions to align with that persona. Here's how:

1. **Strategic Keywords**: Use words in your bio that resonate with the type of match you want to attract. If you're seeking someone adventurous, mention

activities like rock climbing or road trips. Want someone intellectual? Include your favorite book or recent thought-provoking podcast.

2. **Photos That Reflect Your Personality**: Choose photos that visually communicate your interests and lifestyle. For example, a rugged outdoor picture for a sporty vibe or a chic urban setting for sophistication. Match the energy of the type you're hoping to attract.

3. **Bio Customization**: Be upfront about your goals. If you're seeking a relationship with a creative type, mention your love for art galleries or indie films. Want someone confident and assertive? Highlight how you value ambition and drive.

4. **Swiping Patterns**: The algorithm learns from your behavior. If you exclusively swipe right on certain archetypes (e.g., edgy profiles with tattoos or profiles that emphasize travel), you'll see more of those profiles. Being selective helps refine the app's suggestions.

5. **Frequent Updates**: Refresh your profile regularly. This not only keeps your profile active in the app's rankings but also shows that you're serious about connecting. Algorithms often favor recently updated profiles over stagnant ones.

Maximizing Interaction to Master the System

Once your profile is optimized, your interactions will further guide the algorithm. Here are some actionable strategies to boost your visibility and match quality:

1. **Engage Consistently**: Regularly logging in and swiping signals to the algorithm that you're an

active user. Algorithms prioritize active users in the match queue, increasing your chances of being seen by others.

2. **Open Conversations Quickly**: Initiate conversations with new matches within the first 24 hours. High engagement levels show interest and help the algorithm rank higher in search results.

3. **Be Selective but Open-Minded**: While being picky can refine your matches, occasionally engaging with profiles outside your usual preferences introduces variety and helps the algorithm recalibrate for unexpected compatibility.

4. **Respond Promptly**: Quick responses to messages signal to the algorithm that you're engaged and serious. Active communicators are often shown to more active profiles, ensuring higher-quality matches.

5. **Use Paid Features Strategically**: Tools like boosts or super likes can temporarily elevate your visibility. Use them during peak app activity times (usually evenings or weekends) for maximum impact.

Fine-Tuning Preferences for Better Matches

Don't be afraid to experiment with your preferences to see how they affect your matches. Here's how to adapt your settings and behaviors to optimize results:

1. **Expand Location Settings**: Increasing your distance radius can bring in a wider pool of matches, especially if you live in a less populated area. Use this to explore connections you might otherwise miss.

2. **Broaden Age Ranges**: If your preferences are too narrow, the algorithm might struggle to find suitable matches. Loosening these restrictions gives the algorithm more room to work and introduces diversity to your options.
3. **Reassess Your Preferences**: Periodically review and adjust what you're looking for. If certain traits aren't yielding good results, consider tweaking your criteria to align with what's genuinely compatible.
4. **Avoid Over-Swiping**: Indiscriminately swiping right on everyone confuses the algorithm. Be intentional about who you engage with to refine its suggestions and ensure better matches over time.
5. **Revisit Connections**: Sometimes, promising matches are buried under new interactions. Revisit older conversations or unmatched profiles that don't align with your goals to streamline your interactions.

Key Takeaways to Master the Algorithm

- **Authenticity Wins**: The more correct and honest your profile is, the better the algorithm can match you with someone truly compatible.
- **Activity Fuels Visibility**: Regular use, consistent messaging, and engaging interactions keep your profile in the algorithm's favor.
- **Feedback Helps**: Adjust preferences and behaviors based on the quality of matches you receive. Don't hesitate to experiment.
- **Understand Your Target Audience**: Know the type of person you're looking for and tailor your profile to attract them specifically.

By mastering the dating app algorithm with these strategies, you can shift the odds in your favor and maximize your chances of finding meaningful connections. Dating apps may use data to guide you, but your personal approach and authenticity ultimately determine the success of your journey.

Above all, practice patience. Building meaningful connections takes time. Don't be afraid to date someone ugly. Stay optimistic and trust the process, remembering that the journey is as valuable as the destination.

CHAPTER 2 CRAFTING THE PERFECT ONLINE PROFILE

Part 1: The Art of First Impressions

Your profile's photos are the first thing others notice and always'sassure they're high-quality and varied, showcasing your hobbies and personality and if you got it show it. Smiling and keeping eye contact in your pictures conveys warmth and approachability.

Craft a bio that's concise yet engaging. Share memorable anecdotes instead of generic hobbies. For instance, "I once tried baking macarons and ended up with colorful hockey pucks" is far more intriguing than "I like baking,and cats"

Tailor your profile to the app's audience. Platforms like Bumble cater to meaningful connections, while others may focus on casual encounters. Updating your profile regularly signals active engagement, keeping it fresh and relevant.

Part 2: Showcasing Your Unique Value

Highlighting your individuality is essential. Incorporate humor to make your profile memorable. For instance, "I can name every constellation but still get lost in IKEA" invites playful interactions.

Leverage app features like prompts to add depth and conversation starters. Be open yet keep an air of mystery to encourage deeper conversations.

Ultimately, your profile should represent the best version of yourself, attracting the right people while fostering meaningful connections.

CHAPTER 3 NAVIGATING ONLINE DATING INTERACTIONS

Part 1: Crafting the First Message

The first message sets the tone for your interaction, making it crucial to get it right. Avoid generic openers like "Hi" or "How's it going?" Instead, personalize your message by referencing something specific from their profile. For example, "I saw you love hiking—what's your favorite trail?" shows genuine interest and invites a response.

Keep your tone light and friendly. Humor can be a great icebreaker but ensure it's appropriate and considerate. A playful comment about a shared interest can make your message stand out without crossing boundaries.

Be concise yet engaging. Overloading your first message with too much information can feel overwhelming. Aim for a balance that piques curiosity and encourages them to reply.

Ask open-ended questions to foster conversation. Questions like "What's the most unexpected thing that's happened to you this week?" create opportunities for storytelling and deeper engagement.

Lastly, don't be discouraged by silence. Not every match will respond, and that's okay. Focus on the connections that do spark meaningful interactions, and don't take rejections personally.

Part 2: Building Connection Through Communication

Once the conversation is flowing, keep the momentum going with active listening. Pay attention to their responses and reference details they've shared. This shows you're engaged and value their input.

Share about yourself to balance the dialogue. Vulnerability fosters trust, so don't hesitate to reveal your interests, goals, and quirks. Authenticity makes for richer, more meaningful exchanges.

Humor can keep the conversation lively. Light-hearted jokes or witty banter can create a sense of ease and fun. Just be mindful to match their tone and comfort level.

Don't rush to meet in person. Take time to build rapport and set up a level of trust. When the time feels right, suggest a casual meeting in a safe, public space to transition the relationship offline.

Finally, keep respect and patience throughout your interactions. Everyone's pace is different, and being considerate of their boundaries fosters a positive dating experience for both parties.

CHAPTER 4: BUILDING GENUINE RELATIONSHIPS ONLINE

Part 1: Foundations of Genuine Connection

Building genuine relationships online begins with authenticity. When you present your true self, you attract partners who value and align with who you are. Start by openly sharing your values, interests, and goals. For example, if you're passionate about animal welfare, mentioning your volunteer work at a local shelter can spark meaningful connections.

Active listening is a cornerstone of any strong relationship. In online dating, this means paying attention to your match's messages, responding thoughtfully, and asking questions that show genuine interest. It's easy to overlook details in casual chats but focusing on what your match shares builds rapport.

Consistent communication fosters trust. Whether it's a daily check-in or sharing stories about your day, creating a rhythm helps your connection feel steady and reliable. Over time, these small gestures can evolve into a deeper sense of partnership.

Shared activities can strengthen bonds even in an online context. For instance, planning virtual date nights—like watching a movie together or playing an online game— adds depth to your interactions. These moments mimic real-life experiences and help bridge the digital divide.

Honesty is non-negotiable. Misrepresenting yourself might lead to short-term success but will ultimately undermine your connection. Be upfront about your intentions and expectations to avoid misunderstandings and ensure both parties are on the same page.

Part 2: Overcoming Challenges in Online Relationships

Navigating online relationships comes with unique hurdles, but a proactive approach can make all the difference. One common challenge is managing expectations. Not every conversation will lead to a romantic connection, and that's okay. Accepting this reality allows you to approach each interaction with an open mind.

Another challenge is dealing with miscommunication. Text-based conversations lack tone and body language, which can lead to misunderstandings. When conflicts arise, address them directly and seek clarification. A simple, "Can you help me understand what you mean?" can diffuse tension.

Balancing vulnerability and boundaries are crucial. While sharing your thoughts and feelings is important, it's equally essential to protect your emotional well-being. Take your time to build trust before delving into deeply personal topics.

Online dating often involves juggling multiple matches, which can be overwhelming. Focus on quality over quantity. Prioritize connections that feel promising and invest your energy where it truly matters.

Finally, celebrate progress, no matter how small. Whether it's a meaningful conversation or scheduling your first video call, acknowledging these steps helps maintain enthusiasm and momentum in your online relationship journey.

CHAPTER 5 OVERCOMING REJECTION WITH RESILIENCE

Part 1: Understanding the Nature of Rejection

Rejection is a universal aspect of online dating, and learning to navigate it with resilience is essential. It's important to remember that rejection is not always personal. Sometimes, it's simply a matter of compatibility or timing rather than a reflection of your value as a person. Adopting this perspective can help ease the sting and keep your confidence.

Reframing rejection as a learning opportunity is a powerful mindset shift. Each experience, whether positive or negative, provides insights into your preferences and strengthens your resilience. Instead of seeing rejection as a dead-end, view it as a stepping stone toward finding the right connection.

Ghosting, a common phenomenon in online dating, can be particularly disheartening. Understanding that ghosting often stems from a lack of communication skills or clarity on the other person's part—rather than a flaw in you—can help you let go of the frustration and move on.

It's essential to address the emotions that rejection stirs up. Suppressing feelings of disappointment or sadness can lead to burnout. Instead, give yourself space to process the experience and then refocus on what you want to achieve.

Finally, taking breaks from dating apps when rejection feels overwhelming is a healthy practice. Stepping away allows you to recharge, gain perspective, and return to the process with renewed energy and optimism.

Part 2: Building Resilience and Confidence

Developing resilience in online dating starts with a strong sense of self-worth. Take time to show and embrace your strengths, talents, and unique qualities. When you know your value, rejection feels less like a blow and more like a mismatch.

A growth mindset is essential. Treat each interaction, even unsuccessful ones, as opportunities to learn and grow. Reflecting on what worked and what didn't in your approach can help you improve and refine your dating strategy.

Surrounding yourself with a supportive network can also bolster your confidence. Friends and loved ones provide valuable perspective, helping you stay grounded and reminding you of your worth during tough times.

Self-care plays a crucial role in keeping emotional balance. Whether it's through exercise, hobbies, or relaxation techniques, nurturing your mental and physical health keeps you in a positive mindset.

Lastly, focus on the bigger picture. Rejection is a natural part of the journey to finding a meaningful connection. Patience and perseverance will guide you toward the right person, making the process worthwhile.

CHAPTER 6: LONG-DISTANCE RELATIONSHIPS: BRIDGING THE GAP

Part 1: Building a Strong Foundation Across Distances

Long-distance relationships require trust, communication, and effort from both partners. The physical separation can be challenging, but setting clear expectations can help ease the strain. Discuss how often you'll communicate and plan visits to maintain a sense of connection.

Digital tools are invaluable for LDRs. Video calls, shared calendars, and messaging apps enable you to stay close despite the distance. Scheduling regular virtual date nights can replicate in-person experiences and keep the romance alive.

Consistency is key to a successful long-distance relationship. Establishing a routine for calls or messages creates stability and strengthens your bond. Knowing when to expect communication reduces anxiety and fosters trust.

Deep, meaningful conversations are essential. While casual chats are great, delving into personal goals, fears, and dreams helps keep emotional intimacy. This kind of vulnerability strengthens your connection over time.

Shared goals can give your relationship direction. Whether it's planning a future trip or discussing long-term aspirations, having mutual objectives helps you stay united despite the miles between you.

Part 2: Overcoming Challenges in Long-Distance Love

Loneliness is one of the biggest challenges in LDRs. Filling your time with fulfilling activities, hobbies, or friendships can make the absence of your partner more bearable. Staying engaged with your own life prevents feelings of isolation.

Jealousy and insecurities can arise in long-distance relationships. Open communication about your feelings and reassuring one another can help address these emotions before they become barriers.

The lack of physical touch can be difficult to cope with. While virtual interactions can't replace in-person affection, sending thoughtful gifts or handwritten letters can bridge the gap and show your partner they're on your mind.

Time zones and busy schedules can complicate communication. Flexibility and patience are essential to navigate these hurdles. Compromising on times for calls or adapting to each other's routines shows commitment to the relationship.

Reunions are exciting but can also be overwhelming. Manage your expectations and focus on enjoying the moment rather than striving for perfection. These visits are milestones in your relationship, so cherish them without pressure.

CHAPTER 7: COMBATING SWIPE FATIGUE AND REDISCOVERING JOY

Part 1: Recognizing and Addressing Swipe Fatigue

Swipe fatigue is a real phenomenon in the world of online dating, where endless scrolling through profiles leaves users feeling drained and uninspired. If you find yourself swiping mindlessly or dreading the process, it's time to reassess your approach. The first step is acknowledging the burnout and giving yourself permission to take a break.

Sometimes, stepping away from the apps for a week or two can recharge your mindset.

Revisiting your profile and preferences can be refreshing. Over time, your priorities may change, and adjusting your criteria can renew your excitement for meeting new people. Experiment with being more specific or open-minded in your matches to see different results.

Diversifying your dating approach can help combat swipe fatigue. Trying niche apps or engaging in offline dating opportunities, such as joining a club or attending singles' events, can reignite your enthusiasm for connecting with others. Expanding your horizons often brings unexpected possibilities.

Shifting your mindset is another powerful tool. Rather than viewing dating as a chore, consider it an opportunity for self-discovery and personal growth. Each interaction, even if it doesn't lead to romance, offers valuable insights into yourself and others.

Lastly, set boundaries around your app usage. Establishing specific times for swiping or limiting the number of profiles you view each day prevents overexposure and keeps the experience enjoyable. Dating should feel like an adventure, not a job.

Part 2: Rediscovering Joy in the Dating Process

Finding joy in dating starts with self-care. Engage in activities that boost your confidence and happiness, such as exercising, pursuing hobbies, or spending time with loved ones. A strong sense of self makes you more open to meaningful connections.

Celebrate small victories along the way. Whether it's a great conversation or a promising new match, acknowledging positive moments keeps your spirit high. Dating is a journey, and every step forward deserves recognition.

Injecting fun into the process is key. Plan creative dates or message potential matches with playful icebreakers. Bringing humor and spontaneity into your interactions makes them more memorable and enjoyable for both parties.

Focus on authenticity rather than perfection. Trying too hard to impress can feel exhausting, but being genuine attracts the right kind of people. Letting your quirks shine through makes the experience more fulfilling and less stressful.

Finally, remember the bigger picture. Dating isn't just about finding "the one"—it's about learning, growing, and enjoying the process. Keeping an open heart and mind ensures that the experience stays rewarding, regardless of the outcome.

CHAPTER 8: AVOIDING CATFISHING IN ONLINE DATING

Part 1: Spotting the Red Flags

Catfishing, the act of creating a fake online persona to deceive others, is a risk in digital dating. Recognizing red flags early can protect you from emotional and financial harm. Start by examining profiles closely. A lack of detailed information or an overabundance of perfect-looking photos can be signs of a fabricated identity.

Pay attention to inconsistencies in their story. If their messages don't align with their profile or they avoid answering specific questions, proceed with caution. Trust your intuition when something feels off.

Beware of rushed intimacy. Catfishers often try to build a deep emotional connection quickly to manipulate their target. Take your time and let relationships progress naturally, verifying details along the way.

A refusal to meet in person or video chat is another major warning sign. Genuine users are typically open to face-to-face interactions, even virtually. Hesitation or avoidance in this area should raise doubts.

Lastly, protect your personal and financial information. Scammers often exploit trust to request money or sensitive details. Maintaining boundaries and exercising skepticism can prevent costly mistakes.

Part 2: Staying Safe in the Online Dating World

Transparency is key to avoiding catfishing. Share clear and current photos of yourself and expect the same from your match. Apps with verification features can help confirm someone's identity.

Choose platforms with strong security measures. Research apps to ensure they have active moderation and user reporting tools. Reliable platforms prioritize user safety and take reports of suspicious behavior seriously.

Use reverse image searches to verify profile pictures. Tools like Google Image Search can reveal if a photo has been stolen or used elsewhere online. This simple step can save you from potential deceit.

Communicate openly about your comfort level and boundaries. A genuine match will respect your preferences and won't pressure you for personal details. Honest dialogue creates a safer and more trusting connection.

Finally, report suspicious profiles to the app. Alerting moderators not only protects you but also helps prevent others from falling victim to scams. Your vigilance contributes to a safer online dating community.

CHAPTER 9: ALIGNING EXPECTATIONS FOR STRONGER CONNECTIONS

Part 1: The Importance of Clear Communication

Clear communication is the foundation of any successful relationship, especially in online dating. Misaligned expectations can lead to misunderstandings and disappointment, so it's essential to discuss intentions early. Whether you're looking for a causal connection or a long-term partnership, honesty about your goals ensures both parties are on the same page.

Take the time to listen actively. Understanding your match's perspective allows you to assess compatibility and build rapport. Asking thoughtful questions about their values and aspirations helps uncover shared goals and potential challenges.

Establishing boundaries is equally important. Setting clear guidelines for communication frequency, exclusivity, and emotional intimacy creates a framework for a healthy relationship. Respecting these boundaries fosters trust and mutual respect.

Discussing deal-breakers can prevent future conflicts. Being upfront about non-negotiables, such as lifestyle choices or family plans, allows both parties to make informed decisions about continuing the relationship.

Finally, be adaptable. While clear expectations are essential, it's also important to remain open to growth and compromise. Relationships evolve, and flexibility can strengthen your connection as you navigate life's changes together.

Part 2: Building Long-Term Compatibility

Aligning expectations involves exploring compatibility in multiple areas, from values and beliefs to lifestyle preferences. Assessing these factors early helps find potential challenges and areas of alignment. A strong foundation of shared principles increases the likelihood of a successful partnership.

Emotional compatibility is another key part. Understanding each other's communication styles and emotional needs fosters a deeper connection. Being mindful of how you express affection, handle conflict, and offering support strengthens your bond.

Practical compatibility matters too. Differences in career goals, financial habits, or living arrangements can strain a relationship. Discussing these topics openly and working toward solutions prevents future friction.

Building trust is a continuous process. Aligning expectations doesn't mean everything will always go smoothly, but it does provide a roadmap for resolving issues together. Honest dialogue and mutual effort create a resilient and lasting partnership.

Ultimately, aligning expectations is about creating a shared vision for the future. By communicating openly, respecting each other's boundaries, and working together, you can build a relationship rooted in trust, understanding, and love.

CHAPTER 10: FINDING BALANCE BETWEEN DATING AND LIFE

Part 1: Prioritizing Your Well-Being While Dating

Balancing dating and personal life can feel overwhelming, but keeping harmony is essential for long-term success. The first step is recognizing that dating should complement your life, not consume it. A fulfilling personal life provides the foundation for healthy relationships.

Set clear boundaries for dating. Appoint specific times to browse profiles, send messages, or go on dates. This ensures you don't neglect your work, hobbies, or friendships while pursuing love. Time management is key to striking a balance.

Self-care is a cornerstone of balance. Engaging in activities that recharge your energy and boost your confidence enhances your overall well-being. When you feel good about yourself, you bring positivity into your interactions and relationships.

Learning to say "no" is equally important. Not every match or opportunity will align with your goals or schedule, and that's okay. Polite decline allows you to focus on what truly matters without spreading yourself too thin.

Finally, keep your priorities in check. Reflect regularly on what you want from dating and how it fits into your life. Adjusting your approach as needed ensures that your pursuit of love stays both rewarding and manageable.

Part 2: Integrating Dating into a Busy Lifestyle

A busy lifestyle doesn't have to hinder your dating journey. With the right strategies, you can integrate romance into your routine without feeling overwhelmed. Start by using technology to save time. Apps with smart algorithms and scheduling features help streamline the process.

Consider incorporating dating into your existing activities. For example, invite a match to join you for a hobby you enjoy, such as hiking or attending a workshop. This creates meaningful experiences while respecting your schedule.

Communication is key to managing expectations. Let potential matches know about your commitments and availability early on. Honesty fosters understanding and prevents misunderstandings down the line.

Efficiency doesn't mean rushing. Take the time to evaluate matches and connections thoughtfully. Quality interactions are more valuable than frequent but shallow conversations.

Lastly, celebrate small wins. Whether it's a great conversation or a promising date, acknowledging progress keeps you motivated and reminds you why you embarked on this journey. Balancing dating and life may take effort, but the rewards are worth it.

CHAPTER 11: LOVE, PATIENCE, AND ALGORITHMS

Part 1: Embracing Patience in Online Dating

Patience is one of the most overlooked virtues in online dating, yet it's critical for success. The digital age has conditioned us for instant gratification, but meaningful connections take time. Recognizing this can transform your approach and help you remain optimistic even when progress feels slow.

Online dating algorithms are powerful tools, but they are not magic. It's important to understand that the matches they suggest are based on probabilities, not guarantees. Each connection is a chance to learn, grow, and refine your understanding of what you are looking for in a partner.

Frustration often arises when expectations don't align with reality. If a profile seems promising but doesn't lead to a meaningful conversation, it's not a failure. Instead, view each interaction as a stepping stone, bringing you closer to the person who truly complements you.

Patience also allows for better decision-making. Rushing into relationships or overlooking red flags can lead to unnecessary heartbreak. Taking the time to evaluate compatibility ensures that your investment of time and energy is focused on meaningful connections.

Lastly, patience fosters personal growth. The process of dating is as much about self-discovery as it is about finding a partner. By embracing the journey, you develop a stronger sense of your values, desires, and emotional needs.

Part 2: Applying Algorithms with Heart

Algorithms are incredible tools for filtering options and suggesting matches, but they must be complemented by human intuition and effort. While an algorithm can find potential compatibility, it's up to you to explore those connections and bring them to life.

Understanding how algorithms work can empower you. Most dating platforms use criteria like location, interests, and communication patterns to suggest matches. Being honest in your profile and consistent in your interactions helps the algorithm do its job effectively.

It's also crucial to balance data-driven insights with emotional intelligence. A match might tick all the algorithmic boxes but lack the spark that makes a relationship thrive. Trust your instincts and be willing to explore beyond the numbers.

Don't be afraid to adjust your preferences. Algorithms are not static; they adapt to the information you provide. Updating your profile, experimenting with different filters, or broadening your search criteria can lead to unexpected and exciting connections.

Ultimately, love requires a combination of science and serendipity. While algorithms can guide you, they are only part of the equation. The magic happens when two people meet, connect, and build something meaningful together.

www.ingramcontent.com/pod-product-compliance
Lightning Source LLC
LaVergne TN
LVHW051752050326
832903LV00029B/2876